The Tiny Teddies' Picnic

Story by Jackie Tidey
Photography by Lindsay Edwards

Meg and Mum are going
to the park for a picnic.

The tiny teddies are going, too.

"Tiny teddies," said Meg.

"We are at the park."

Red Teddy

is not in Meg's basket!

"Here is the picnic," said Mum.

Meg looked at the tiny teddies.

"Oh, no!" said Meg.

"Where is Red Teddy?

He is not here!"

"Come and look in the car

for Red Teddy,"

said Mum.

Meg ran to the car.

"Red Teddy!" cried Meg.
"Where are you?"

Meg looked down
in the leaves.

"Mum!" said Meg.

"Here is Red Teddy."

"Come to the picnic, Red Teddy,"
said Meg.